Who Am I?

by Wiley Blevins

Reading Consultant: Wiley Blevins, M.A.
Phonics/Early Reading Specialist

COMPASS POINT BOOKS

Minneapolis, Minnesota

Compass Point Books
3109 West 50th Street, #115
Minneapolis, MN 55410

Visit Compass Point Books on the Internet at *www.compasspointbooks.com*
or e-mail your request to *custserv@compasspointbooks.com*

Photographs ©: Cover: Index Stock/Ralf-Finn Hestoft p. 1: Index Stock/Ralf-Finn Hestoft,
p. 6: Corbis/Ed Bock, p. 7: Corbis, p. 8: Index Stock/Kent Knutson, p. 9: USDA/ARS/Bruce
Fritz p. 10: Index Stock/Zephyr Pictures, p. 11: Corbis/Bob Krist, p. 12: top left: Unicorn
Stock/Aneal Vohra, p. 12: top right: Corbis, p. 12: bottom left: RubberBall Productions/Mark
Andersen, p. 12: bottom right: Corbis

Editorial Development: Alice Dickstein, Alice Boynton
Photo Researcher: Wanda Winch
Design/Page Production: Silver Editions, Inc.

Library of Congress Cataloging-in-Publication Data
Blevins, Wiley.
  Who am I? / by Wiley Blevins.
    p. cm. — (Compass Point phonics readers)
  Summary: Shows people dressed for work in an easy-to-read text that
  incorporates phonics instruction and rebuses.
  Includes bibliographical references and index.
    ISBN 0-7565-0534-8 (hardcover : alk. paper)
  1. Occupations—Juvenile literature. 2. Reading—Phonetic
  method—Juvenile literature. [1. Occupations. 2. Rebuses. 3.
  Reading—Phonetic method.] I. Title. II. Series.
    HB2581.B58 2003
    331.7—dc21   2003006380

Table of Contents

Dear Parent or Caregiver,

Welcome to Compass Point Phonics Readers, books of information for young children. Each book concentrates on specific phonic sounds and words commonly found in beginning reading materials. Featuring eye-catching photographs, every book explores a single science or social studies concept that is sure to grab a child's interest.

So snuggle up with your child, and let's begin. Start by reading aloud the Mother Goose nursery rhyme on the next page. As you read, stress the words in dark type. These are the words that contain the phonic sounds featured in this book. After several readings, pause before the rhyming words, and let your child chime in.

Now let's read *Who Am I?* If your child is a beginning reader, have him or her first read it silently. Then ask your child to read it aloud. For children who are not yet reading, read the book aloud as you run your finger under the words. Ask your child to imitate, or "echo," what he or she has just heard.

Discussing the book's content with your child:

Explain to your child that in a community, people have different jobs. Some people work in offices. Others work outside. Some people wear uniforms to work. Have your child share what he or she knows about people who work in your community.

At the back of the book is a fun Word Bingo game. Your child will take pride in demonstrating his or her mastery of the phonic sounds and the high-frequency words.

Enjoy Compass Point Phonics Readers and watch your child read and learn!

Jack Sprat

Jack Sprat
Could eat no **fat,**
His wife could eat no lean;
And so between them both,
They licked the platter clean.

I am a .

I am a firefighter.

I am a vet .

I am a .

I am a  teacher .

I am a .

Who am I?

Word List

Short *a*

am

f

farmer

firefighter

m

musician

t

teacher

High-Frequency

a

I

who

Word Bingo

You will need:
- 1 sheet of paper
- 18 game pieces, such as pennies, beans, or checkers

Player 1

farmer	a	I
who	mat	at
fat	am	teacher

How to Play

- Fold and cut a sheet of paper into 10 pieces. Write each game word on one of the pieces. The words are *a, I, am, mat, fat, who, at, farmer, teacher, firefighter*.
- Fold each piece of paper and put it in a bag or box.
- The players take turns picking a folded paper and reading the word aloud. Each player then covers the word if it appears on his or her game card. The first player to cover 3 words either down, across, or on the diagonal wins. You can also play until the whole card is covered.

Player 2

am	mat	fat
teacher	who	a
at	firefighter	I

Read More

Flanagan, Alice K. *Teachers*. Community Workers Series. Minneapolis, Minn.: Compass Point Books, 2001.

Miller, Heather. *Firefighter*. This Is What I Want to Be Series. Chicago, Ill.: Heinemann Library, 2002.

Owen, Ann (ed.) and Sandra D'Antonio (illustrator). *Old MacDonald Had a Farm*. Minneapolis, Minn.: Picture Window Books, 2003.

Schaefer, Lola M. *We Need Mail Carriers*. Mankato, Minn.: Pebble Books, 2002.

Index